Smithsonian

SMITHSONIAN MUSEUM FUN!

Dinosaur Tall and Dinosaur Small

Finding Opposites at the Museum

by Christianne Jones

PEBBLE
a capstone imprint

Published by Pebble, an imprint of Capstone
1710 Roe Crest Drive, North Mankato, Minnesota 56003
capstonepub.com

Copyright © 2025 by Capstone. All rights reserved. No part of this publication may be reproduced in whole or in part, or stored in a retrieval system, or transmitted in any form or by any means, electronic, mechanical, photocopying, recording, or otherwise, without written permission of the publisher.

The name of the Smithsonian Institution and the sunburst logo are registered trademarks of the Smithsonian Institution. For more information, please visit www.si.edu.

Library of Congress Cataloging-in-Publication Data
is available on the Library of Congress website.
ISBN: 9780756582470 (hardcover)
ISBN: 9780756582425 (paperback)
ISBN: 9780756582432 (ebook PDF)

Summary: Join Sammy the tour guide and look for opposites at a natural history museum.

Editorial Credits
Editor: Christianne Jones; Designer: Jaime Willems; Media Researcher: Svetlana Zhurkin; Production Specialist: Whitney Schaefer

Special thanks to Matthew T. Miller, Museum Specialist, National Museum of Natural History. Capstone would also like to thank the following at Smithsonian Enterprises: Avery Naughton, Licensing Coordinator; Paige Towler, Editorial Lead; Jill Corcoran, Senior Director, Licensed Publishing; Brigid Ferraro, Vice President of New Business and Licensing; Carol LeBlanc, President

The author would like to thank Gina Ostrowski for her consulting expertise.

Image Credits
Alamy: Corbin17, 23 (left); Capstone: Jon Hughes, cover (right); Dreamstime: Jiawangkun, 14 (right), Travis Rogers, 18 (left); Getty Images: Orla, 18 (right), 27, Science Photo Library/Mark Garlick, 6 (right), 14 (left), 26, Science Photo Library/Roger Harris, 12 (left), 26, Stocktrek Images/Corey Ford, 22 (left), 27, Stocktrek Images/Elena Duvernay, 21 (right), 23 (right), 27, Stocktrek Images/Mohamad Haghani, 7 (right back), 15, 20, 26, 27, Stocktrek Images/Robert Fabiani, 17, 26, Stocktrek Images/Roman Garcia Mora, 25, 27, Stocktrek Images/Sergey Krasovskiy, 30, 31; Newscom: Xinhua/Bao Dandan, 9 (left); Science Source: Masato Hattori, 10 (left front), 26; Shutterstock: Agung Surya, 13 (right back), 26, Alberto Andrei Rosu, 10 (left back), 24, 26, 27, Daniel Eskridge, 16, 26, Elenarts, 29 (right), kan_khampanya, 12 (right), Matthew Dicker, 22 (right), Michael Rosskothen, 11 (back), 28 (left), Nsit, cover (top), back cover (top), 1 (top), ochikosan (bone background), cover, back cover, rodos studio Ferhat Cinar, 8 (left), 26, schusterbauer, 29 (left), Sebastian Kaulitzki, 7 (right front), 13 (right front), 26, Sergii Figurnyi, 3, Ton Bangkeaw, 28 (right), travelershigh, 13 (left), tynyuk (guide), 4 and throughout, Victor1153, 8 (right), Visual Generation, 4 (fossils), Warpaint, 9 (right), 11 (front), 19, 26, 27; The Smithsonian Institution: National Museum of Natural History, 7 (left); Svetlana Zhurkin: cover (left), back cover, 5, 6 (left), 10 (right), 21 (left)

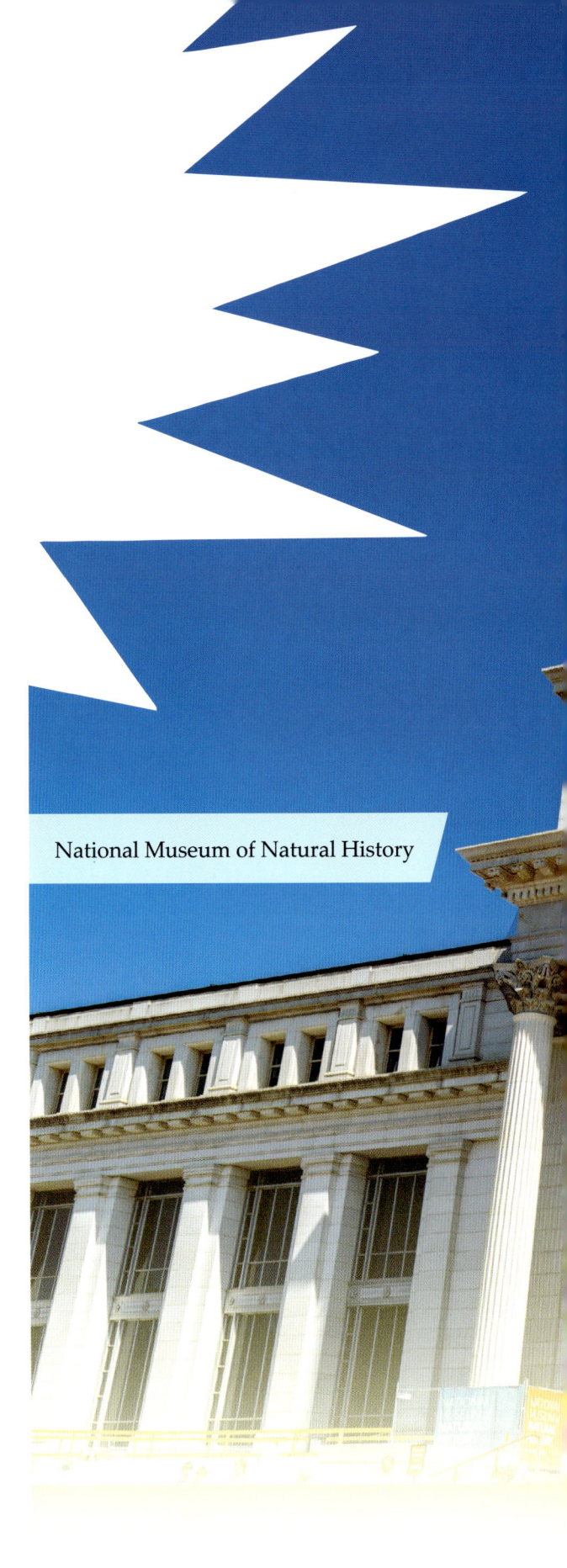

National Museum of Natural History

Printed and bound in China. PO 6096

Dinosaurs and many other prehistoric animals no longer roam the earth, but you can still see them at a museum.

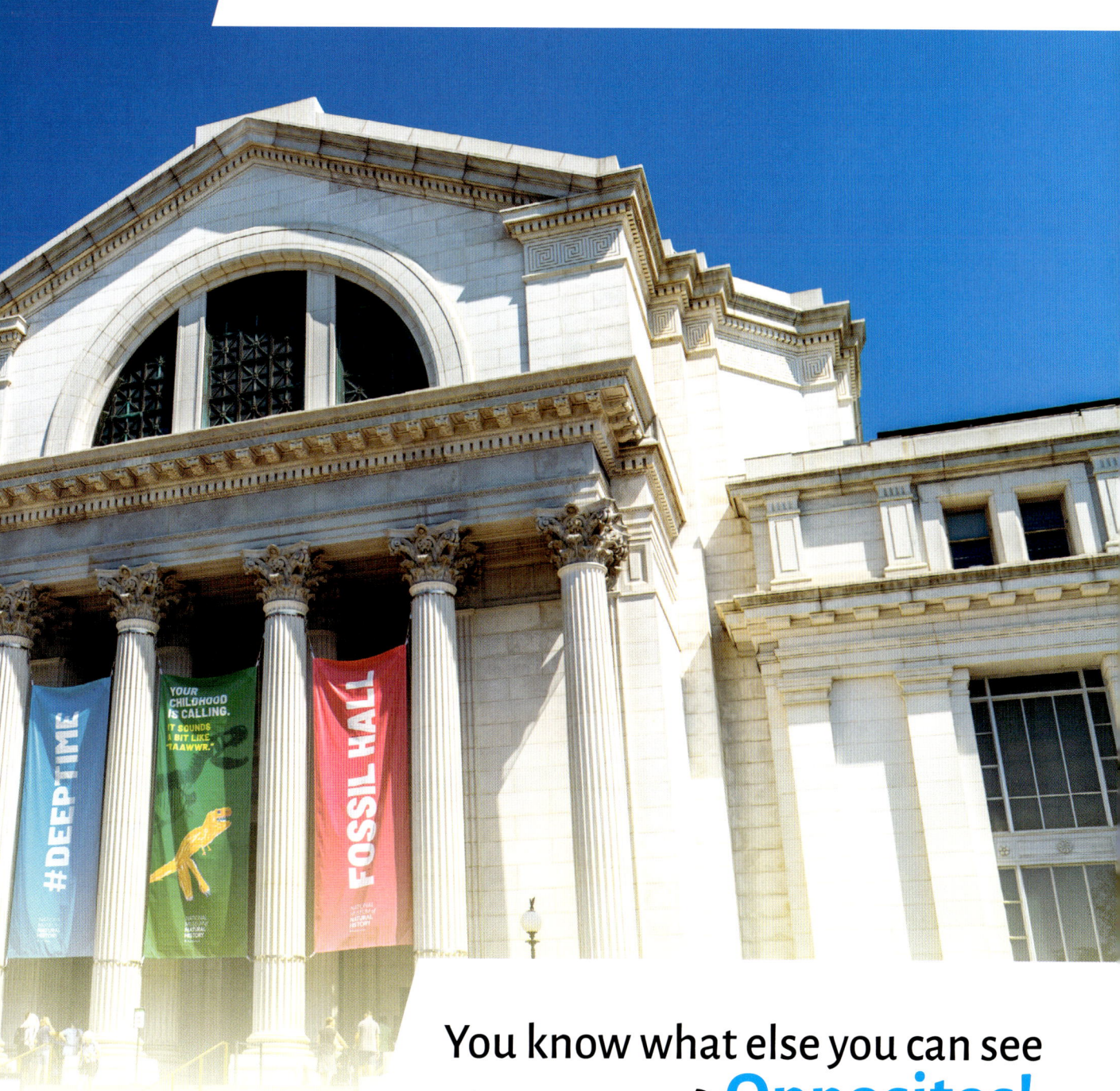

You know what else you can see at a museum? **Opposites!**

Meet our tour guide, Sammy. She is a paleontologist, so she knows a lot about dinosaurs and other prehistoric animals.

paleontologist
a scientist who studies fossils

Let's explore the museum and find opposites together. Listen closely to Sammy during our tour. She might just try and trick you!

Sammy says the Diplodocus has a **SHORT** neck.
Is Sammy being silly or serious?

Silly! The Diplodocus has a **LONG** neck.

The Edmontosaurus has a **SHORT** neck.

Pronunciation Guide
Edmontosaurus ed-MON-toe-SAWR-us
Diplodocus di-PLO-duh-kus

Sammy says the Iguanodon has **SHARP** teeth.
Is Sammy being silly or serious?

Silly! The Iguanodon has **DULL** teeth.

The Spinosaurus has **SHARP** teeth.

Pronunciation Guide
Iguanodon ih-GWAN-o-dahn
Spinosaurus SPY-nuh-SAWR-us

Sammy says the Sinosauropteryx is a **SMALL** dinosaur. Is Sammy being silly or serious?

Serious! What is the opposite of **SMALL**?

BIG! The Titanosaurus is a **BIG** dinosaur.

Pronunciation Guide
Sinosauropteryx SY-no-sawr-OP-ter-iks
Titanosaurus tahy-TAN-uh-SAWR-us

Sammy says the Mosasaur is swimming **BELOW** the water. Is Sammy being silly or serious?

A Mosasaur is not a dinosaur. It is an extinct reptile.

Serious! What is the opposite of **BELOW**?

ABOVE! The Pterodactylus can fly **ABOVE** the water.

A Pterodactylus isn't a dinosaur. It is another extinct reptile.

Pronunciation Guide

Mosasaur MOH-suh-SAWR

Pterodactylus tair-uh-DAK-tuhl-us

Sammy says the Triceratops has **THIN** legs.
Is Sammy being silly or serious?

Silly! The Triceratops has **THICK** legs.

The Velociraptor has **THIN** legs.

Pronunciation Guide
Triceratops tri-SER-uh-tops
Velociraptor vuh-LOSS-eh-RAP-tur

Sammy says the Ankylosaurus has a **BUMPY** back.
Is Sammy being silly or serious?

Serious! What is the opposite of **BUMPY**?

SMOOTH! The Allosaurus has a SMOOTH back.

Pronunciation Guide
Ankylosaurus ANG-koh-lo-SAWR-us
Allosaurus AL-uh-SAWR-us

Sammy says it looks like the Tyrannosaurus Rex is moving **SLOW**. Is Sammy being silly or serious?

Silly! The Tyrannosaurus Rex is moving **FAST**.

It looks like the Torosaurus is moving **SLOW**.

Pronunciation Guide
Tyrannosaurus Rex tie-RAN-uh-SAWR-us REX
Torosaurus TOR-uh-SAWR-us

Sammy says the Albertosaurus's mouth is **OPEN**.
Is Sammy being silly or serious?

Serious! What is the opposite of **OPEN**?

CLOSED! The Centrosaurus's mouth is CLOSED.

Pronunciation Guide
Albertosaurus al-BURR-toe-SAWR-us
Centrosaurus SEN-tro-SAWR-us

Sammy says the Parasaurolophus is **IN** the water.
Is Sammy being silly or serious?

Serious! What is the opposite of **IN**?

OUT! The Edaphosaurus is **OUT** of the water.

The Edaphosaurus is actually an extinct reptile, not a dinosaur.

Pronunciation Guide
Parasaurolophus PAR-uh-SAWR-oh-LOH-fus
Edaphosaurus ed-uh-fuh-SAWR-us

Sammy says the Brachiosaurus is **SHORT**. Is Sammy being silly or serious?

Silly! The Brachiosaurus is **TALL**.

Variraptors are SHORT.

Pronunciation Guide
Brachiosaurus BRACK-ee-uh-SAWR-us
Variraptor VA-ree-RAP-tor

With Sammy's help, we found lots of opposites at the museum.

SHARP

LONG

DULL

SHORT

SMALL

BELOW

ABOVE

BIG

THICK

BUMPY

SMOOTH

THIN

FAST

SLOW

OPEN

CLOSED

IN

OUT

SHORT

TALL

Good work! Sammy didn't trick you at all.

What's the oppposite of **HELLO?**

Styracosaurus

Pronunciation Guide
Styracosaurus stie-RAK-o-SAWR-us
Apatosaurus a-PAT-uh-SAWR-us

GOODBYE!

Apatosaurus

Spot the 5 DIFFERENCES

1. no volcano smoke
2. color of the dinosaur plates changed
3. a Pterodactylus is missing in the sky
4. dinosaur in the right corner is missing teeth
5. feathered dinosaur added in lower left corner

Dinosaur Dig

There are thirteen bones hidden in this book. Dig back in and see if you can find them. What's the opposite of STOP? **GO!**

Opposite Extras

We dug up ten opposite pairs on our museum visit. Can you complete twelve more pairs of opposites?

1. top and ?
2. empty and ?
3. up and ?
4. heavy and ?
5. soft and ?
6. wet and ?
7. hot and ?
8. loud and ?
9. near and ?
10. narrow and ?
11. true and ?
12. beginning and ?

Three of the extinct creatures in this book are NOT dinosaurs. Can you name them?